# THE LITTLE ENGINEER COLORING BOOK

# CARS AND TRUCKS

# BY SETH MCKAY

The Little Engineer Coloring Book: Cars and Trucks by Seth McKay
www.TheLittleEngineerBooks.com

Copyright © 2018 by Seth McKay

For permissions contact:
permissions@TheLittleEngineerBooks.com

ISBN: 9781791613501

# Table of Contents

Introduction (*for Parents*) ...................................................................... v

Introduction (*for the Little Engineers*) ................................................ vi

Tips on Using this Book ......................................................................... vii

The First Cars ........................................................................................... 1

The First Trucks ....................................................................................... 2

Car Types .................................................................................................. 3

Where Cars are Made ............................................................................. 4

Car Frame ................................................................................................. 5

Engine ....................................................................................................... 6

Engine Cylinder ....................................................................................... 7

What a Gas Engine Needs ..................................................................... 8

Diesel Engines ......................................................................................... 9

How Many Cylinders? ........................................................................... 10

The Engine Block ................................................................................... 11

Parts on the Engine Block ................................................................... 12

Engine Accessories ............................................................................... 13

Radiator .................................................................................................. 14

Superchargers and Turbochargers .................................................... 15

Superchargers ........................................................................................ 16

Turbochargers ........................................................................................ 17

Twin Turbochargers .............................................................................. 18

Electric Motors ...................................................................................... 19

Supercars with Electric Motors .......................................................... 20

Front, Mid and Rear Engine ...................................................... 21

Transmission ........................................................................... 22

Driveshaft .............................................................................. 23

Differential ............................................................................. 24

4-Wheel Drive ........................................................................ 25

How 4WD Works .................................................................... 26

2 Differentials ........................................................................ 27

4x4 ........................................................................................ 28

Front Wheel Drive .................................................................. 29

Suspension ............................................................................ 30

Solid Axle vs. Independent Suspension .................................. 31

Steering ................................................................................. 32

Tires ...................................................................................... 33

Wheels ................................................................................... 34

Brakes .................................................................................... 35

Lights ..................................................................................... 36

Power Windows ...................................................................... 37

Windshield Wipers .................................................................. 38

Inside the Car ......................................................................... 39

Instrument Cluster .................................................................. 40

How Do Cars Get Fuel? .......................................................... 41

Electric Car Recharge ............................................................. 42

BONUS: Free Digital Copy ...................................................... 43

Special Preview! Space and Rockets Coloring Book ................ 44

# Introduction *(for parents)*

Thank you so much for your interest in The Little Engineer coloring books. In these books, your child will be introduced to new, interesting topics and begin to understand how things work.

I've always wanted my children to understand how things work, and in general, understand that objects are not magical boxes that work for some unknown reason. I want them to understand that objects are quite simple when broken down into a few key components. Without any direction, it is possible for a child to get the wrong understanding of objects that we consider to be simple.

For example, we understand that a printer has a roller that moves the paper and a little ink jet that sprays the paper with ink as it rolls by to make images. However, it would be very easy for our children to see the same printer and conclude that this magic box shoots out paper, and this is where paper comes from.

I chose to make this book a coloring book because I wanted to ensure that the book was also fun! I don't want this book to be too serious, boring or overwhelming. Coloring helps keep the book fun while incorporating new and challenging topics.

## Book Objective:

The objective of this book is not to make your child an engineer (I hope your child chooses whatever career path suits him or her best), and the objective is not for your child to know exactly how everything works and memorize each part of a car.

The objective is simply to begin to introduce your child to new, interesting concepts that might catch his or her attention and help your child understand that seemingly complex things are just a few simple items put together.

# **Introduction** *(for the Little Engineers)*

Hello Little Engineer!

My name is Seth, and I'm the Chief Engineer of this book. We will have so much fun learning about different parts of a car.

We will start with some of the first cars ever made and see what those look like. We will talk about all the main parts of a car and even super cool parts like turbochargers and new electric motors.

Enjoy coloring, ask your parents lots of questions, and most of all have fun!

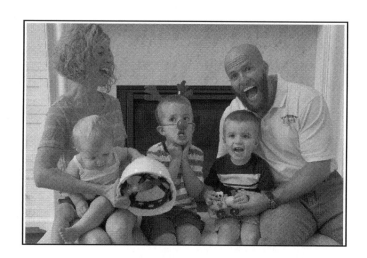

# Tips on Using this Book

- **Read the book to your child** – Before coloring the book, read it one time to help your child get a sense of the "big picture" before they focus on a single page to color.

- **Add your own explanations** – You know your child best so take the wording on a page and expand on it to help your child understand.

- **Relate the pages to your surroundings** – As you and your child walk around, point out different features on cars or ask them to help you find the items on a vehicle. (For example, ask them to show you the differential on a vehicle.)

- **Use your own car as an example** – Ask your child if they want to see specific parts on your car. This will help them get a sense of how these parts look "in the real world." Warning: If you've just driven the car, many parts will be too hot to touch so be careful and don't let your child touch hot car parts.

- **Make use of the digital download** – Once your book is fully colored, be sure to download the file and print another copy so the book can be enjoyed an unlimited amount of times. You may want to keep the original book if your child likes to read through it, and then extra printed pages can be just for coloring.

The Little Engineer Coloring Book: Cars and Trucks

# LET'S GET STARTED!

The Little Engineer Coloring Book: Cars and Trucks

# THE FiRST CARS

THE FIRST VEHICLE WAS MADE ALMOST 250 YEARS AGO!
WOW, THAT IS A LONG TIME AGO. IT HAD 3 WHEELS
AND A STEAM ENGINE, BUT NEVER DROVE VERY FAR.
ABOUT 120 YEARS AGO, WAGONS WITH GASOLINE ENGINES
WERE INVENTED.

*Blank to allow bleed through and use of markers.*

# THE FIRST TRUCKS

TEN YEARS AFTER THE FIRST GAS POWERED CAR,
A TRUCK VERSION WAS MADE THAT WAS MORE POWERFUL
AND COULD CARRY MORE CARGO.

The Little Engineer Coloring Book: Cars and Trucks

# CAR TYPES

**COMPACT**

**SEDAN**

**TRUCK**

**SUV**

**VAN**

**SPORTS CAR**

CARS AND TRUCKS COME IN MANY DIFFERENT SIZES.

HERE ARE SOME OF THE MAIN TYPES:
COMPACT, SEDAN, TRUCK, SUV, VAN, AND SPORTS CAR

The Little Engineer Coloring Book: Cars and Trucks

# WHERE CARS ARE MADE

MOST CARS ARE MADE IN LARGE FACTORIES AND THE
FACTORY MAKES HUNDREDS OF CARS EVERYDAY.
THE CARS ARE THEN DRIVEN ONTO CAR TRANSPORT TRUCKS,
TRAINS OR BOATS AND TAKEN ALL AROUND THE WORLD.

The Little Engineer Coloring Book: Cars and Trucks

# CAR FRAME

FRAME

ENGINE

TRANSMISSION

DRIVESHAFT

FUEL
TANK

DIFFERENTIAL

AXLE

WHEEL

MOST CARS ARE BUILT ON A FRAME.

THE FRAME IS MADE OF METAL AND IS VERY STRONG
SO THAT IT CAN HOLD ALL THE HEAVY PARTS OF THE CAR
LIKE THE ENGINE, TRANSMISSION, SUSPENSION AND
THE BODY OF THE CAR.

The Little Engineer Coloring Book: Cars and Trucks                                        *Blank to allow bleed through and use of markers.*

# ENGINE

THE ENGINE IS ONE OF THE MOST IMPORTANT PARTS OF A CAR. THE ENGINE HAS MOVING PARTS THAT MAKE THE WHEELS SPIN SO THE CAR MOVES. SOME ENGINES ARE POWERED BY DIESEL FUEL WHILE OTHERS USE GAS (ALSO CALLED  GASOLINE). SOME CARS HAVE ELECTRIC MOTORS INSTEAD OF GAS OR DIESEL ENGINES.

The Little Engineer Coloring Book: Cars and Trucks

# ENGINE CYLINDER

SPARK PLUG

EXHAUST

FUEL + AIR

PISTON

CONNECTING ROD

CRANKSHAFT

AN ENGINE HAS 1 OR MORE CYLINDERS IN IT. EACH CYLINDER HAS A PISTON INSIDE OF IT THAT MOVES UP AND DOWN WHICH MAKES THE CRANKSHAFT SPIN. THE CRANKSHAFT IS CONNECTED TO THE WHEELS, AND MAKES THE WHEELS SPIN TOO. THE PISTON MOVES BECAUSE FUEL GOES INTO THE CYLINDER AND MAKES A SMALL EXPLOSION WHEN THE SPARK PLUG LIGHTS THE FUEL ON FIRE.

The Little Engineer Coloring Book: Cars and Trucks

# WHAT A GAS ENGINE NEEDS

A GAS ENGINE NEEDS 3 THINGS TO WORK:
AIR, FUEL AND A SPARK.

- AIR GOES THROUGH THE AIR FILTER AND INTO THE ENGINE.
- A FUEL PUMP PUSHES THE GAS FROM THE GAS TANK TO THE ENGINE.
- SPARK PLUGS MAKE A SPARK. THE SPARK PLUGS NEED POWER SO THEY ARE CONNECTED TO THE BATTERY FOR ELECTRICITY.

*Blank to allow bleed through and use of markers.*

# DiESEL ENGiNES

DIESEL ENGINES ONLY NEED AIR AND FUEL TO OPERATE.
A DIESEL ENGINE SQUEEZES THE AIR AND FUEL SO TIGHT IN
THE CYLINDER THAT THE FUEL EXPLODES BY ITSELF!
NO SPARK PLUG NEEDED.

MOST BIG TRUCKS HAVE DIESEL ENGINES BECAUSE
THE ENGINES ARE VERY POWERFUL AND CAN HELP
CARRY HEAVY LOADS.

## QUESTION TIME!

A GAS V8 ENGINE HAS 8 SPARK PLUGS.
HOW MANY SPARK PLUGS DOES A DIESEL V8 ENGINE HAVE?

The Little Engineer Coloring Book: Cars and Trucks

*Blank to allow bleed through and use of markers.*

# HOW MANY CYLINDERS?

V4

V6

V8

i6

ENGINE NAMES ARE USUALLY BASED ON HOW MANY CYLINDERS THE ENGINE HAS.

A V8 ENGINE HAS 8 CYLINDERS.
AN I6 ENGINE HAS 6 CYLINDERS. IT IS ALSO CALLED AN INLINE 6 BECAUSE ALL THE CYLINDERS ARE IN A LINE.

## QUESTION TIME!

HOW MANY CYLINDERS DOES A V6 ENGINE HAVE?

The Little Engineer Coloring Book: Cars and Trucks

# THE ENGINE BLOCK

TOP OF A PISTON

CYLINDERS

THE ENGINE BLOCK IS A BIG METAL PART WITH "HOLES" IN IT FOR EACH CYLINDER. THE PISTONS, CONNECTING RODS AND CRANKSHAFT ARE HIDDEN INSIDE OF THE ENGINE.

## QUESTION TIME!

HOW MANY CYLINDERS CAN YOU SEE?

# PARTS ON THE ENGINE BLOCK

INTAKE MANIFOLD

EXHAUST MANIFOLD

CYLINDER HEADS

OIL FILTER

MANY PARTS GO ON TOP OF THE ENGINE BLOCK.
CYLINDER HEADS COVER UP THE CYLINDER "HOLES."
AN AIR INTAKE MANIFOLD IS ADDED ON TOP OF THE ENGINE.
ALL THE AIR THAT GOES INTO THE CYLINDERS GOES THROUGH
THE INTAKE MANIFOLD FIRST. THE EXHAUST MANIFOLDS
CONNECT THE ENGINE TO THE EXHAUST PIPES THAT GO
UNDER THE CAR.

The Little Engineer Coloring Book: Cars and Trucks

# ENGINE ACCESSORIES

BELT

AC COMPRESSOR

POWER STEERING PUMP

ALTERNATOR

THE ENGINE ACCESSORIES ARE POWERED BY A BELT ON THE ENGINE. THE BELT SPINS THE WHEELS ON THE ACCESSORIES WHEN THE ENGINE IS ON.

- THE ALTERNATOR IS THE BATTERY CHARGER FOR THE CAR. IT IS A SMALL POWER GENERATOR THAT MAKES SURE YOUR CAR HAS PLENTY OF ELECTRICITY FOR LIGHTS, SPARK PLUGS, THE RADIO AND MORE.

- THE AC COMPRESSOR HELPS THE AC SYSTEM WORK SO THE AIR IS NICE AND COLD INSIDE THE CAR.

- THE POWER STEERING PUMP MAKES IT EASIER TO TURN THE STEERING WHEEL.

The Little Engineer Coloring Book: Cars and Trucks

# RADIATOR

HOT COOLANT

RADIATOR

COLD COOLANT

**ENGINES GET VERY HOT.**

- A RADIATOR HELPS KEEP THE ENGINE FROM GETTING TOO HOT.
- A WATER PUMP MOVES A SPECIAL LIQUID CALLED COOLANT THROUGH THE ENGINE AND THEN THROUGH A RADIATOR.

The Little Engineer Coloring Book: Cars and Trucks

# SUPERCHARGERS AND TURBOCHARGERS

AiR

SUPERCHARGERS AND TURBOCHARGERS ACT LIKE A FAN
THAT PUSHES EXTRA AIR INTO THE ENGINE.

THE EXTRA AIR ALLOWS THE ENGINE TO HAVE MORE POWER
SO THE ENGINE CAN MAKE THE CAR GO EVEN FASTER!

*Blank to allow bleed through and use of markers.*

# SUPERCHARGERS

SUPERCHARGER

BELT THAT SPINS SUPERCHARGER

SUPERCHARGERS ARE FANS THAT ARE POWERED BY A BELT THAT SPINS WHEN THE ENGINE IS ON.

MOST SUPERCHARGERS ARE ON TOP OF THE ENGINE AND SOMETIMES IT IS SO BIG THAT YOU CAN SEE IT STICKING OUT OF THE HOOD!

The Little Engineer Coloring Book: Cars and Trucks

# TURBOCHARGERS

## TURBOCHARGER

AIR GOING IN ENGINE

EXHAUST COMING OUT OF ENGINE

A TURBOCHARGER IS NOT POWERED BY A BELT. INSTEAD, IT IS LIKE A 2 SIDED FAN. THE EXHAUST SHOOTING OUT OF THE ENGINE SPINS ONE SIDE OF THE FAN SO THIS SPINS THE OTHER SIDE OF THE FAN WHICH PUSHES AIR INTO THE ENGINE.

The Little Engineer Coloring Book: Cars and Trucks

# TWIN TURBOCHARGERS

## TURBOCHARGERS

### THIS CAR HAS 2 TURBOCHARGERS!

MOST TURBOCHARGERS ARE UNDER THE HOOD AND HARD TO SEE, BUT SOME CARS HAVE THEM STICKING OUT OF THE HOOD WHICH IS REALLY COOL!

The Little Engineer Coloring Book: Cars and Trucks

# ELECTRIC MOTORS

CARS ALSO USE ELECTRIC MOTORS. ELECTRIC MOTORS HAVE LESS MOVING PARTS WHICH HELPS THEM LAST LONGER.

THE MOTORS IN AN ELECTRIC CAR ARE POWERED BY BATTERIES. MOST REMOTE CONTROL CARS WORK THE SAME WAY!

The Little Engineer Coloring Book: Cars and Trucks

*Blank to allow bleed through and use of markers.*

# SUPERCARS WiTH ELECTRIC MOTORS

## SOME OF THE FASTEST SUPERCARS IN THE WORLD HAVE ELECTRIC MOTORS!

The Little Engineer Coloring Book: Cars and Trucks

*Blank to allow bleed through and use of markers.*

# FRONT, MID AND REAR ENGINE

**FRONT**

**MID**

**REAR**

THERE ARE FRONT, MID AND REAR ENGINE CARS.

- FRONT ENGINE CARS HAVE THE ENGINE BETWEEN THE FRONT WHEELS AND THE FRONT OF THE CAR.

- MID ENGINE CARS HAVE THE ENGINE BETWEEN THE FRONT AND REAR WHEELS.

- REAR ENGINE CARS HAVE THE ENGINE BETWEEN THE BACK WHEELS AND BACK OF THE CAR.

The Little Engineer Coloring Book: Cars and Trucks

*Blank to allow bleed through and use of markers.*

# TRANSMISSION

ENGINE

TRANSMISSION

THE TRANSMISSION CONNECTS TO THE BACK OF THE ENGINE.

THE TRANSMISSION HAS DIFFERENT GEARS THAT HELP THE WHEELS SPIN AT THE RIGHT SPEED. THE TRANSMISSION ALSO HAS A GEAR CALLED 'REVERSE' SO THE CAR CAN MOVE BACKWARDS.

The Little Engineer Coloring Book: Cars and Trucks

*Blank to allow bleed through and use of markers.*

# DRIVESHAFT

THE BACK OF THE TRANSMISSION IS CONNECTED TO A
DRIVESHAFT WHICH IS CONNECTED TO THE DIFFERENTIAL.
THE DIFFERENTIAL AND AXLE ARE CONNECTED
TO THE WHEELS SO THAT THE WHEELS SPIN WHEN THE
DRIVESHAFT SPINS.

The Little Engineer Coloring Book: Cars and Trucks

# DiFFERENTiAL

## DiFFERENTiAL

THE DIFFERENTIAL NEEDS TO BE VERY STRONG TO
HANDLE ALL THE ENGINE'S POWER. YOU CAN SEE THE
DIFFERENTIAL BETWEEN THE BACK WHEELS OF MOST
TRUCKS. IT IS THE ROUND PART IN THE MIDDLE OF THE
AXLE.

# 4-WHEEL DRIVE

IN MANY VEHICLES, ONLY THE BACK WHEELS SPIN WHICH IS CALLED "2-WHEEL DRIVE." SOME CARS AND TRUCKS HAVE "4-WHEEL DRIVE" WHICH MEANS THAT ALL 4 WHEELS ARE CONNECTED TO THE ENGINE. THIS ALLOWS THE VEHICLE TO DRIVE IN MUD OR OVER BIG ROCKS AND NOT GET STUCK.

The Little Engineer Coloring Book: Cars and Trucks

*Blank to allow bleed through and use of markers.*

# HOW 4WD WORKS

IN A 4-WHEEL DRIVE VEHICLE, A TRANSFER CASE IS ON THE BACK OF THE TRANSMISSION AND THIS CONNECTS TO THE FRONT AND REAL AXLES. THIS ALLOWS THE ENGINE TO SPIN THE FRONT AND BACK WHEELS.

The Little Engineer Coloring Book: Cars and Trucks

# 2 DIFFERENTIALS

REAR
DIFFERENTIAL

FRONT
DIFFERENTIAL

ON TRUCKS, YOU CAN SOMETIMES SEE 2 DIFFERENTIALS.
THIS MEANS THE TRUCK HAS 4-WHEEL DRIVE.
SOME CARS HAVE 4-WHEEL DRIVE, BUT IT IS HARD
TO SEE THE DIFFERENTIAL BECAUSE THE CAR IS
CLOSE TO THE GROUND.

The Little Engineer Coloring Book: Cars and Trucks

*Blank to allow bleed through and use of markers.*

# 4X4

4X4 SYMBOL

4x4

4X4 MEANS THE SAME THING AS 4-WHEEL DRIVE. IF YOU
CAN'T SEE THE FRONT DIFFERENTIAL, YOU CAN LOOK FOR
THE "4X4" SYMBOL TO SEE IF A TRUCK IS 4-WHEEL DRIVE.

The Little Engineer Coloring Book: Cars and Trucks

*Blank to allow bleed through and use of markers.*

# FRONT WHEEL DRIVE

SOME 2-WHEEL DRIVE CARS ONLY POWER THE FRONT WHEELS; THIS IS CALLED FRONT WHEEL DRIVE.

The Little Engineer Coloring Book: Cars and Trucks

*Blank to allow bleed through and use of markers.*

# SUSPENSION

SUSPENSION CONNECTS THE WHEELS TO THE FRAME OR BODY OF THE CAR. THE SUSPENSION CAN MOVE UP OR DOWN AS THE CAR GOES OVER BUMPS TO HELP KEEP THE TIRES ON THE ROAD.

*Blank to allow bleed through and use of markers.*

# SOLID AXLE VS. INDEPENDENT SUSPENSION

**INDEPENDENT SUSPENSION**

**SOLID AXLE**

INDEPENDENT SUSPENSION ALLOWS EACH WHEEL TO MOVE UP AND DOWN ON ITS OWN (OR INDEPENDENTLY). A SOLID AXLE IS LIKE A STRAIGHT LINE THAT CONNECTS BOTH WHEELS SO THE WHEELS MOVE UP AND DOWN TOGETHER.

The Little Engineer Coloring Book: Cars and Trucks

*Blank to allow bleed through and use of markers.*

# STEERING

THE STEERING WHEEL IS CONNECTED TO THE FRONT 2 WHEELS; TURNING THE STEERING WHEEL ALLOWS THE DRIVER TO CONTROL WHERE THE VEHICLE GOES. A MONSTER TRUCK HAS REAR STEERING, SO THE REAR WHEELS CAN TURN TOO!

The Little Engineer Coloring Book: Cars and Trucks

# TiRES

TIRES ARE THE BLACK RUBBER PART ON THE OUTSIDE OF THE WHEEL. TIRES ARE VERY IMPORTANT. A TIRE IS THE ONLY PART OF THE CAR THAT TOUCHES THE GROUND. TIRES HAVE SPECIAL GROOVES FOR WATER OR DIRT SO THAT THE WHEEL CAN TOUCH THE ROAD EVEN ON RAINY DAYS.

The Little Engineer Coloring Book: Cars and Trucks

*Blank to allow bleed through and use of markers.*

# WHEELS

TIRE

WHEEL

THE WHEEL IS THE METAL PART THAT CONNECTS TO THE CAR. WHEELS ARE USUALLY SILVER BUT CAN BE ANY COLOR.

*Blank to allow bleed through and use of markers.*

# BRAKES

BRAKE CALIPER

ROTOR

WITH WHEEL OFF

CALIPER

ROTOR

THE BRAKES STOP THE CAR. PUSHING THE BRAKE PEDAL MAKES THE BRAKE CALIPERS SQUEEZE THE ROTORS TO SLOW THE CAR DOWN. BRAKES ON A BIKE WORK THE SAME WAY.

The Little Engineer Coloring Book: Cars and Trucks

*Blank to allow bleed through and use of markers.*

# LiGHTS

- HEADLIGHTS IN THE FRONT OF THE CAR LIGHT UP THE ROAD ON DARK NIGHTS.
- TAIL LIGHTS HELP TO MAKE SURE OTHER PEOPLE SEE THE CAR.
- BRAKE LIGHTS WARN OTHERS THAT THE CAR IS SLOWING DOWN, SO THEY'LL NEED TO SLOW DOWN TOO.

The Little Engineer Coloring Book: Cars and Trucks

*Blank to allow bleed through and use of markers.*

# POWER WINDOWS

WINDOW GLASS

WINDOW MOTOR

POWER COMES FROM BATTERY IN CAR

WINDOW REGULATOR

WINDOW SWITCH

THERE IS A MOTOR IN THE DOOR THAT MOVES THE WINDOWS UP AND DOWN. THE WINDOW SWITCH SENDS ELECTRICITY FROM THE BATTERY TO THE MOTOR WHICH MAKES THE MOTOR MOVE THE WINDOW.

The Little Engineer Coloring Book: Cars and Trucks

*Blank to allow bleed through and use of markers.*

# WINDSHIELD WIPERS

WINDSHIELD
WIPER

WINDSHIELD
CLEANING FLUID

WINDSHIELD
WIPER MOTOR

WINDSHIELD WIPERS CLEAN OFF THE WINDSHIELD
ON RAINY DAYS.
THERE IS A MOTOR THAT SPINS THE WIPERS.
THERE IS ALSO A TANK OF CLEANING FLUID IN THE CAR
THAT WILL SQUIRT ONTO THE WINDSHIELD
WHEN THE DRIVER PUSHES A BUTTON.

The Little Engineer Coloring Book: Cars and Trucks

*Blank to allow bleed through and use of markers.*

# INSIDE THE CAR

GEAR SHIFTER

RADIO

AIR CONDITIONING CONTROLS

STEERING WHEEL

## THE DRIVER CAN CONTROL MANY THINGS FROM THE DRIVER SEAT.

- THE STEERING WHEEL CONTROLS WHERE THE CAR GOES.
- THE GEAR SHIFT CONTROLS WHICH GEAR THE TRANSMISSION IS IN.
- THE RADIO CONTROLS THE SOUNDS COMING OUT OF THE SPEAKERS.
- THE AIR CONDITIONING CONTROLS DETERMINE HOW HOT OR COLD IT IS INSIDE THE CAR.

*Blank to allow bleed through and use of markers.*

# iNSTRUMENT CLUSTER

- **FUEL GAUGE:** SHOWS HOW MUCH FUEL IS IN THE TANK.
- **SPEEDOMETER:** SHOWS HOW FAST THE CAR IS GOING.
- **TACHOMETER:** SHOWS HOW FAST THE ENGINE IS SPINNING.
- **ENGINE TEMPERATURE:** SHOWS THE TEMPERATURE OF THE ENGINE.

The Little Engineer Coloring Book: Cars and Trucks

# HOW DO CARS GET FUEL?

CARS FILL UP THEIR GAS TANKS AT THE GAS STATION.
GAS STATIONS HAVE HUGE TANKS UNDERGROUND
THAT HOLD ALL THEIR FUEL.
TANKER TRUCKS DELIVER FUEL TO THE GAS STATION TANKS.

*Blank to allow bleed through and use of markers.*

# ELECTRIC CAR RECHARGE

ELECTRICITY GOING INTO
THE CAR TO CHARGE BATTERIES

AN ELECTRIC CAR DOESN'T HAVE A GAS TANK. IT HAS
A BIG BATTERY AND THE BATTERY IS CHARGED WITH A
PLUG IN THE GARAGE. SOME PARKING LOTS ALSO HAVE
CHARGING STATIONS SO ELECTRIC CARS CAN CHARGE UP
WHILE PARKED AT A STORE.

The Little Engineer Coloring Book: Cars and Trucks

# Free Digital Copy

Go to www.thelittleengineerbooks.com/carstrucks-digital-download or scan the QR code, and enter your email to get a ready-to-print PDF.

Feel free to use this download when you are done with the book so your child can use the coloring book again and again.

**Please be kind and do not distribute your digital copy. Thank you!**

# SPECIAL PREVIEW

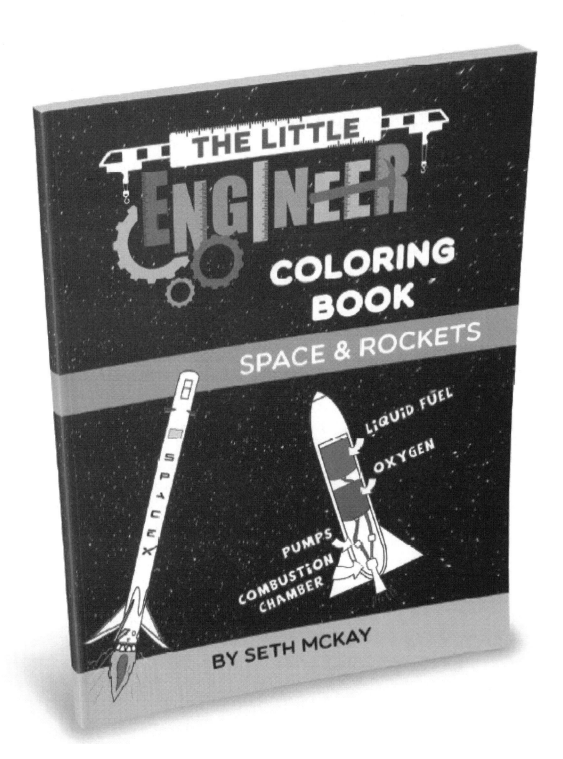

*Check out this short preview of another fun coloring book!*

# THE SOLAR SYSTEM

## THE EARTH IS IN THE SOLAR SYSTEM.
## OUR SOLAR SYSTEM CONSISTS OF THE SUN
## AND 8 PLANETS.

The Little Engineer Coloring Book: Cars and Trucks

# GOING TO THE MOON
## STEP 3

## STEP 3: FIRE STAGE 3 OF THE ROCKET TO LEAVE EARTH'S ORBIT AND HEAD TOWARD THE MOON.

*Blank to allow bleed through and use of markers.*

# LAUNCH STAGES

3RD STAGE
ROCKETS

2ND STAGE
ROCKETS

1ST STAGE
ROCKETS

## THE ROCKET HAS SEVERAL DIFFERENT SECTIONS CALLED STAGES.

The Little Engineer Coloring Book: Cars and Trucks

*Blank to allow bleed through and use of markers.*

# SPACEX
# HOW THE ROCKET LANDS

ONCE THE 1ST STAGE OF THE ROCKET SEPARATES
FROM THE 2ND STAGE, THE 2ND STAGE WILL
CONTINUE TOWARDS ORBIT, BUT THE 1ST STAGE
THEN TURNS AROUND AND FLIES BACK TOWARDS
A LANDING SPOT ON EARTH.

The Little Engineer Coloring Book: Cars and Trucks

*Blank to allow bleed through and use of markers.*

# MODERN ROCKETS

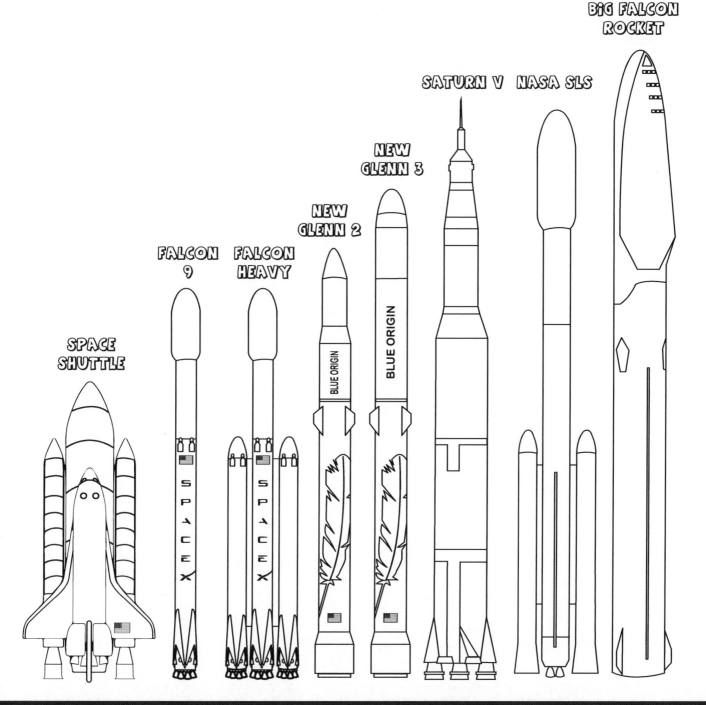

BIG FALCON
ROCKET

SATURN V    NASA SLS

NEW
GLENN 3

NEW
GLENN 2

FALCON    FALCON
9         HEAVY

SPACE
SHUTTLE

BLUE ORIGIN

BLUE ORIGIN

SPACEX

SPACEX

# THERE ARE CURRENTLY MANY NEW ROCKETS JUST BECOMING AVAILABLE. THE SATURN V AND SPACE SHUTTLE ARE INCLUDED JUST FOR COMPARISON.

The Little Engineer Coloring Book: Cars and Trucks

I hope you enjoyed the book!
Contact me anytime at TheLittleEngineerBooks.com
if you have any questions or suggestions for a new book
you would like to see.

Feedback is always great!
Consider leaving a review online if you have time.

Chief Engineer: Seth
TheLittleEngineerBooks.com
TheLittleEngineerBooks

Made in the USA
San Bernardino, CA
14 April 2020